Time as Distance

Mark Halperin

New Issues Poetry & Prose

A Green Rose Book
Selected by Nancy Eimers

New Issues Poetry & Prose
The College of Arts and Sciences
Western Michigan University
Kalamazoo, MI 49008

First Edition, 2001

ISBN: 0-932826-21-0 (paperbound)

Library of Congress Cataloging-in-Publication Data:
Halperin, Mark
Time as Distance/Mark Halperin
Library of Congress Catalog Card Number (00-132574)

Art Direction: Tricia Hennessy
Design: Ivo Gasparotto
Production: Paul Sizer
                    The Design Center, Department of Art
                    College of Fine Arts
                    Western Michigan University
Printing: Courier Corporation

Time as Distance

Mark Halperin

New Issues

WESTERN MICHIGAN UNIVERSITY

Also by Mark Halperin

for B.

Contents

Time as Distance

I

Millennium

Maybe a change of number can transform
  a life: aren't the resolutions we make
at the start of each new year, new birthday,
  decade, century, millennium, marks
of that wild hope, more frayed each time?
      Do our tracks narrow like eyes
converging toward our vanishing beliefs?

Say we didn't count and lived as we imagine
  animals do, in the continuous present,
no more conditioned by past than future.
  Would that be less odd than invisible
crevasses cutting off this week from that—
      our rounding temporal corners?
Did Zeno get it wrong? Is it lack of motion

that confutes time, not shifts in speed and/or
  direction? Does the mind seek height
the way the body fears falling and earthquake
  fissures that close with us inside? When
some sold their possessions and waited for
      the end a thousand years ago,
others bought them up and spun their wheels

as the earth continued too. Then families
  that wandered out beyond city gates
came drifting back, for work and food, for
  the sorry lives they'd thought to shed
like gravity, forced to resurrect old habits,
      calendars, a useless innocence.
Howls must have rattled the steeple clocks.

Studying Russian

My father's friends, that collection
of raggedy-assed scroungers I thought
he valued because they spoke Russian,
his first language, were more important
than I thought because language was more
than the grammar and words I would struggle at.
There were the street-names, what you saw

looking down from a bridge they all knew,
the smell of soup and wet hides,
wet eyes, the fears you could allude to
over schnapps when, as a point of pride,
you could refuse to admit what the booze
brought home in its fog: that you missed
the dirt, the sullen mob, news

that terrified you, but missed it all
the same because you had escaped
what was gone anyway. Those oddballs
must have vaguely felt the weight
of not being able to talk about it
when they met over the rich syllables
they alone understood as a gift.

Orphans

In Tallinn, in a small town in Pennsylvania,
in Matsue—the lives I cast off like clothes
lie in heaps beside the still warm beds.
I went on somewhere else, here, but the life
I left the way I put down a glass, entering

another room, meaning to come back for it,
still anticipates my hand or body. Maybe
in one of those places a man looks up from
his reading expecting me to enter, or a woman
rounding a corner pauses beside old stones

for a second, thinking it's me crossing the square.
And maybe only the streets wait, only the trees
arching above them. Some mornings, groggy
from sleep, uncertain which life is mine, I turn
as bigamists must, wondering just whose embrace

I will enter. My son has bashed the car door,
my wife glowers. Is one of those lives left
standing open, uncompleted, waving desperately,
discontinued branches, junctions and occasions,
orphaned possibilities only I am missing from?

In Chekhov

In Chekhov, everyone's unhappy—
this one loves that one who loves
someone else. The doctor, a fixture
of the plays, is always old as Chekhov,
who died young, must have felt himself
to be. And the aging writer, who also
resembles Chekhov, chases a girl

he will abandon soon and is stuck
with the habit of drawing out small
notebooks every so often, wanting
the youth he traded for fame. *Moscow,*
say the sisters, *is where we could be
happy*, knowing they will never
get there, too beautiful for happiness,

with feelings too keen, dreams,
like their upswept hair, too outdated—
their long dresses part of history.
Work, says one hero, *love* says another.
No one can tell you if happiness
is anything but the opposite of
irony or being unprotected.

The Muse as Lilith

Though they are cleaner than we are, more
delicate even in the articulation of their joints,
our loves resemble us. If what they ask for
and what they need aren't always the same,
it is our job to sense the latter and provide it.

So only someone come to tempt us would show,
as in the mirror of a lover's face, where we are most
deeply reflected, that no matter what we tell
others, we cannot have love as we want it,
unencumbered by agreements reached silently over the years.

Only someone with no intention of returning
our love would insist that love can be neither gift
nor possession. Like Lilith, that one would
hiss *honesty is only the ruse you use to find or
tolerate yourself.* That one, independent, cold, would show

love in all its swollen, throbbing childishness.
Turn off the lights, the mundane lover says, but the Muse
moves under the lamp, inviting us to inspect more
closely, forcing us nearer, even with passion.
If we court her, crave her visits, call her our ideal,

how could it be with any thought of measuring
others, with any question of body or beauty or comfort?
With the Muse, there is only sorrow, manna
in the desert—a sign that God provides or
our evidence there is no God, though we are provided for.

The Good News

We all know bad news sneaks up
on us like cigarette smoke, the smell of it
hanging in air, clinging to our
hair and the fibers of our clothing weeks after.
A catch in the throat, a dropping
of eyes—the bad news comes as we're
busy congratulating ourselves
on having escaped it, drink in hand,

the moon's slow rise soothing,
cool as a washcloth dipped in water, folded
and laid across a brow. A distant
phone rings. A letter waits primly on the table.
This must be, you think, what
it is to live, like a pale illusion grown
luminously silver, surely this.

How different, coming from beyond our
conception, after we'd forgotten
asking for a passport to the new life, using
the ready terms of exchange
like dollar or peso, new shoes, new car, new
house to embody notions of desire,
when fortuitously, the good news came.
It was a chance to travel, a kind face—

forms that shunned mystery. In tiny streets
you'd been adopted by,
bells braided into the manes of horses rang
when their skins unexpectedly
shivered. Within that followed such privacy
the heel of bread you chewed
was more than all you could want.

Cold Comfort

There's a sprinkling of stars, a wedge of moon
above the walk to the cabin, and cold—
every member of the household
asleep inside. You feel ice sink in,
looking into the infinitely wide,
receding sky, and away from your son,
your dying mother—even your life,
shriveled as its faith in reason.

The voices start: where did you get off
believing you could know enough
to say which paths led where—pure
chutzpah when the world's a shimmer,
a chimera or watery reflection
the winds stir. A boy's sure
his talent for music is something alien.
You'd scream if that helped, roar

and bellow and squeal. What helps is the cold
air here to there, and like an ember's,
a star's faint pulsings
in a puddle of black so remote
it's past imagining. Or nothing
helps except the fatigue which brings
a mother healthy again, and a dream-
worn father, who can draw, through bars, a son.

Waiting

Is it the Leningrad Station's stairs of marble,
  or lined by flower-hawkers and topped
by four huge eagles, the *Kievskij Voksal*,
or are we in Tallinn, by the outside wall
  of gray stone, a clock, a bus-stop
and inside two enormous reader boards
flashing train schedules, every bench full,
babies bawling or sleeping, bundles set
  next to bundles and a bad smell
drifting in from the toilets?

Waiting to leave again, I think: I've become
  one of them: the waiting a person does
here—for others to arrive, for bread, for the one
door of four in the theater that is open,
  for the paper, the milk, the cheese that was
available once, endless lines like a conjugation:
I wait for you, you wait for me—like a phone,
a droning on and on, the Russian shrug,
  the waving as his train pulls out, of a Russian
soldier, the dog on the rug . . .

As we wait, it becomes night, a winter wind
  howling down the chimney and the snore
of the dog a comfort. Darkness seems to bend
around the house and the house to settle scores.
  Shoulders loosen; we seem to mend
with a drink, tension to lessen a bit more.
At home, we can afford the wind. Let it kick up endless
snow and clog the passes, I'm safe, we say, nervous
  when it goes on too long, a little unsure
and afraid of suggestive words

because events have trained us to believe
  in their power and because we've waited
in so many stations for so many people, retrieved
our suitcases now countless times, scraped
  against a chair or a stranger and heaved
sighs of relief between trips, those visited states
including total disorientation and unrelieved
boredom by now. The refuges were little islands
  where we waited, of course, carved our names
and tried to make new friends.

The Elegant Ladies of Tallinn

The elegant ladies of Tallinn
paint their eyelids purple
and wear felt hats with broad brims.
They are slender and the little
bulbs at the ends of their thin
noses twitch when they speak Estonian:

aitah and *uks*, or rarer,
stranger words for *thank-you*
and *one*. The winter sun rises later
than they do and breaks through
the clouds to shadow their fair
skin with icy blue hints of ardor.

Centuries of sea air have mellowed
the narrow streets and cobbles
their high heels totter along, and the yellow,
blue and orange stucco walls
they pass in their long coats,
hats tipped. There, restorers, Poles,

in the fifteenth century houses
of the burghers of Tallinn using shoddy,
imported bricks, survey the crowds
milling below them from rickety
platforms and spy on the proud
ladies of Tallinn. But the ladies have pity

and avoid them like mud or shouting
children with ice-cream. It could seem
nineteen thirty-five again, but without
Hitler to the southwest or Stalin
to the east, as the ladies chat about
news, hoping tomorrow's will find them

under more middle European than Soviet
cloudy skies. They look higher
than where Tallinn's intricate weathervanes pivot—
to "Old Thomas," on the *Raekoda* spire
from the thirteenth century, to his verdict,
as their mothers did and their mothers, and before.

(Spring 1990, Estonia still part of the Soviet Union)

The Swedish Minister at Tartu, 8 Feb 1990

If he hadn't spoken so slowly, hadn't launched himself
with such measured self-assurance into
the history of his family as far back as the battle of
Poltava on his mother's, the short side,
hadn't, with the patience of ministers, asked if I knew
what a chalice was, and righteously explained

three hundred years ago the parish chalice had been lost when
the battalion on his father's side fell as well
as how that very chalice found its way back to his parish
where he was, in his own words, "rooted like an oak,"
maybe his remarks about the old German Jews he'd known
in Israel, with no words to express love,

his sympathy for their estrangement, then in 1972
for Palestinians, feeling as he put it "like a goy"
for the first time in his life, with the disrupted
sense of place and naive assumption I could
share there in the cavernous restaurant we ate in in Tartu,
Estonia, guests among conferring guests: maybe

his own words wouldn't have worked so far down in me
that, though I smiled and repeatedly questioned
him, complimenting his powers of expression, I feel
fortunate now I will never again see the tall
black back and turned collar beneath the expressionless,
pallid face, nor hear that cold voice again.

Easter Lilies

The trumpets that address the three
corners of the room away from me,
the curled lips, lowered bells
and tightly latched buds, tilted
like the heads of speakers about to punctuate
a phrase with this hand or that, repel

and offend me no less than the wrapping paper
around the pot does, silver
inside, outside maroon-metal. The generous
ruffles intimidate then command
the table, the alcove and finally the room
like organ swells. Tall, decorous—

svelte, one is tempted to say, or graceful
as a woman—like a woman, its spell
derives from a mixing of the deliberate
and accidental, though plants can't choose
how they're adorned or the uses they're put to,
not hot-house forcings, not supermarket

items "reduced for immediate purchase,"
and left to say "thanks" with and outlast
a visit. I could like the yellow, yolk-
rich anthers, imagining their pollen
will sift like dust, but the waxy sheen
of the petals affronts me as tokens swollen

with death and hung from a green stem would,
less phalluses than bullets, the way they nod
familiarly, the eerie perfection
of each spreading flower that puffs
out its virginal, spilled-seed perfume,
its aloofness such as saints smile down from.

Yom Kippur Again

Sundown to sundown, I eat nothing, drink
  nothing and let my sins
flap inside me like trapped black birds.
  They are a kind of heart
and hand too, beating my breast for me

and, thus, the sweet fruits of restraint.
  I don't pray or wonder why
we are here leading the imperfect lives
  we're forever wrestling with.
Fasting's a poor man's gesture, empty as

any non-doing or refraining from—to be
  given up when the faster chooses.
At three or four, I edge toward hunger,
  thirst—goaded by forbidden
writing. Red or yellow leaves pull me

through a window, the growl and tightness
  in my bowels they are parts of.
Light scatters and bunches on the foothills,
  mauve in the clefts and traffic
thickening while the drivers shift down,

as if to remind me I've two hours to go.
  It's enough, a small voice
whispers like a hesitant pen, and I begin
  again, confidence renewed. I
could shave with the edge of my hunger,

split a second into a hundred nasty slivers.
  Oh, denial's rich enough to
barter with, if only we knew for what. More
  stinging arguments against what's
partial, I sing, flinging it like a challenge.

$$\frac{22}{23}$$

II

Fathers and Sons

I'm climbing the last rise, high on some hill
of bitterness. When my wife says, you'll want
    visits later, I roar back: I don't care:
everything we didn't do—games he begged
off, times he was too busy with buddies, girls,
    like a shaky flame, insisting:
    I know what I'm doing—
they replaced the past that might have joined us.

I'm wading those watery places, sharp with
their sting of private salt. I'm laying claim to
    anger's suspect eloquence and exasperation,
wanting to hurt, the fuel of explosions waiting for
the right blue spark as night and darkness pool.
    Maybe he hears; maybe my wife
    drops off to sleep at last
and the dog curls up on its little rug to snore.

I check them off the way I lock the doors at night.
My heart rocks its heaviness and my fists
    clench, nothing to close around.

On the Steps of Temple Shalom

Inside the old, gray stone house,
its eaves trimmed in the flat-board,
Midwest style of the neighborhood,
  the children are learning Hebrew
  and history and to be Jewish
as best they can where Jews are few.

Maybe they are learning to be rare
while old snow melts from the roof
and the sun, absent recently, proves
  it can shine in the blue
  and white sky. These are colors
the children would be sure to notice, who

are learning the flag of Israel
and their ties to all that history.
Recognize them? They'd rather be
  screaming and chasing each other,
  instinctively like other children.
And they will soon, but must wait. More

than one of my uncles would have said
Jews can't live in Yakima or
the town we drove from. One would be sure
  we'd never be American
  enough, another terrified
we just might, all of them come

too far not to understand
only the shadow of the past
grows, but thinner, more odorless.
  The children sit in a room
  waiting for their parents
to rescue them from Temple Shalom.

They are further away all the time,
as Temple Shalom is, under its blue
and white skullcap. It weathers the distance
  carried even here, the Jew's
  childlike refusal whose name,
if there is one, like God's, we must not use.

Spinoza

There was only one work, one
picture the parts of which needed to fit
each other, to cohere, and only
that mutual dependence interested him
given the tightness of a web
in which the failure of even one strand,

letting it sag too far in one
direction and then drag and droop or start
to cave in, would seem to require
full knowledge at the start, omniscience,
since, if the pattern that links
the parts is to hold through time it must

escape even temporal boundaries,
a notion fatally like the knowledge that it
will precede its being. And from
that Spinoza shied. There, amid the numbers
that organize his geometrical
exposition, intuition and the love of God,

exotic as winter fruit, hearten
those for whom too much reason stifles and
suffocates, like a speaker implying
that Spinoza lacked a way to describe something
further because here vision exceeded
the language in which it could be embodied.

I do not know. Some hold
the truth is something in the world
words try to describe and others,
the fit of words to the world. Only a few
would say it is the sound of
certain words when they have found each other

after long searching. Calling
something "predestined" only dresses one
mystery in another when we appear
to each other ill-educated salespeople offering
our services, stumblers, liars, trying
to get right what we have not heard said before.

Just the Light

for Phil

The light back on the hills, just
the light, the aspens white,
and in dense patches the changing
brick-red glow and orange
in the chokecherry, lit again
like candles. When clouds hang

above the rural roads, slicing
the hills off, who wouldn't lose
his balance? Before, just with the light
washing us, we were anointed and moved
without effort, gliding into good health
or good digestion or whatever else

we took for granted. But let the gray cape
of its absence drop and we can't escape
feeling robbed, shrunken, so poor
even our attention flees. The earth's a slough,
an enclosure. We ignore
food, windows, and rock as if *davening*

or moored boats. For loyalty,
look to a dog, the bird on the pine tree
for song—creatures with a finer sense
of what it is
to live in all weathers. We love
only the light, how low rays of it slant

though the windows like jets on a bombing run
to explode gloom. There's never enough,
says my friend, who can feel gray
descend, whose grow-lamp is his rabbi.
Like a coyote, he must be gorging with joy
at its return today, wiping it from his eyes.

Prediction

Inveigling fate, straining to stack the deck,
    there are always some who will
try to convince themselves that cheating is *magic*
    aided, a kind of skill
    chance-taking lends them, their personal
gain, the world's good fortune—and news addicts,

who think they know better, staring at TV screens
    on which some delegate, tired
as they, emerges from the peace conference convened
    yesterday while the reporter pries
    behind and into what lies
ahead. But what I want to know is,

when it's easy to know for sure, why listen
    to guesses at all? Isn't
such curiosity a yielding to fear? Champion
    of the obvious, loudmouth of the manifest,
    it's time that I confessed:
I like to keep between now and then. Because

tomorrow arrives or not, by which time it's too
    late to make hay or money
if you didn't have some to start with. Because you
    can name dates, an authority
    by virtue of timing, and not know
when the trees have leafed out, what a late snow

forced the deer in canyons to do. Somewhere
    they want to know what's happening
there, which is here and now or ponds of air;
    and falling vertically in one
    window, aslant in the other,
is a snow so cold you lose at its touch all feeling.

Needs

Bright and charming, the man who asks your help
is planning to use you in ways you won't like
when you find out. He's amusing, calm, except
when he tells you about the young woman
close to his heart. He needs her here. She needs
an "invitation"—for the visa. It turns out

she's his girlfriend. They worked together, went out
after work, he explains—he couldn't help
himself. She's fifteen years his junior. She needs
him. It happens. His former wife understood. *You'd like
them both*. She's more a colleague than a woman
who breaks up marriages. That's all, except

his wife is not his former wife—yet. *Accept
my apologies for the misunderstanding*. It comes out,
actually she works as a typist. *For a woman,
work's hard to find.* He wants you to want to help,
and just by listening, you've agreed to like
him, haven't you? That helps. And maybe you need

to know your name's on the telegram, need
to remember you're in trouble if you don't accept
what he's done, though he doesn't say anything like
that. *Have his university help?* That's out—
his wife works there. Is it clearer now? Friends help:
he's owed some favors, something about a woman . . .

You're better off not knowing more. As for his woman,
the forms require information. You need
her birth date? She's not lazy and could help
with work in the library, he explains—except,
you see, she can't speak English. It turns out,
she's twenty years his junior. What's it like,

you wonder, doling out facts? Are they more like
interest or capital? What will the woman
do here? What will he do with her here without
more friends? Before this all started, whose needs
were whose? When the invitation is accepted
and the visa issued, he tells you: *Your help*

was invaluable. Except for your help
the woman close to me would be without
me. You say, *likewise, I'm sure.* We all have needs.

Abe Lincoln, the First Jewish President

Last year, when a pleasant Estonian, only a little anti-Semitic,
mentioned America's first Jewish President, we were driving to Lahaemaa,
the old estate house at Palmse of one of those Baltic-German barons who
regarded Eastlanders the way the English regarded Chinese—slightly lower
than dogs. My friend, a misplaced Catholic, chatting of Lincoln, then
others, the bankers you'd expect, the Roosevelts, the Rockefellers, was
honestly surprised at my denial. "But his name—it's Old Testament," he
went on, meaning honest Abraham's of course, not Theodore or Franklin,
much less Nelson. The rest of the conversation merely embroidered that
common

anti-Semitism an Australian-Estonian acquaintance admitted was no
Soviet gift, but indigenous, low key since there never had been many Jews
and everyone's favorite Russian, the scholar Lotman, wasn't he a Jew? Why
his son even spoke Estonian and had converted—the sincerest flattery. So
after I set him right about America, that there were no Jewish presidents
and it was, to my knowledge, not run from New York, Tel Aviv or
Jerusalem by some Cabal, I tried to enjoy the remnants of the day, the swan
ponds, the fine furniture and more or less succeeded though I never felt
quite

comfortable with him again. So imagine Jenya, of all people,
repeating it on *Kuznetskij Most*, street of "the blacksmiths' bridge" in
Moscow, Jewish Jenya fighting me as I try to correct her. "And Streisand
and Douglas, not Jewish too," she shrieks back, defiant, incredulous. I was
lost. What do you say when the truth's no help? What storerooms of pride
are you ransacking and in what cause? It took weeks, a month before I
started understanding. It took more walking and more Jenya, notions like
"Slavanski" and cultural, Russian Jews, till slowly, like ice-thickened
vodka, light rushing down like dirty water on both sides of *Kuznetskij
Most*,

which is without blacksmiths or bridges much less a river—I saw at last that, where I was, biblical names aren't for Russians, who get named for the Holy Saints, and that only a Jew would so name a child where it's no small matter to grow up a Moshe or Jacob, an Esther or Sarah. Reminded where I was—in hostile territory—maybe *Kuznetskij Most* arced for a split second and I recalled all the Jews I knew here, Irinas and Alecs and Jenyas. I welcomed him, poor, tormented Abe, with whiskers yet, that long nose and rheumy eyes. What else could he be but Jewish?

Man on the Stairs

I.

As I'm going down, he's racing up the stairs—
red sweatband, green sweatpants, tee-shirt soaked
through from maybe his tenth stair-climb. I look
away from the grizzled cheeks and thinning hair.
He had a wife, a son, a job here. They
left when he was let go. But he would stay,

or the part that climbs stairs would, while the part
with a family disappeared. Even hearts
tire. Maybe that's what he wants, the mindlessness
of shaping up, even if you have to pay
with health. Say he pitied the almost perfect
dull line of my life, his own so richly exotic.

I'd have to follow, track him to know, trick
him into talking, and if he did, pray
I didn't learn more than I wanted to.
Maybe he relies on seeming dangerous—
that keeps the doorways open and the space between us
from collapsing while he fades from view.

II.

Hadn't I seen Conrad hanging a fast
right by the library, sweeping past me, cocked
    hat, brim snapped down—that hangdog,
bulldog face only a week ago? only a month?
    Hadn't I said at breakfast: "shouldn't we
do something," forgot, then let the saying join
    with other rumbles waving for attention—
someone you shared a hallway or boss with,
    you lowered your eyes too contritely
like hats you also feared would blow away.
    But the drabness of the notice—
friends may sign a guestbook at the mortuary—
    was definitive as guilt. Some editor
of the local paper had him loving books,
    family, adventure—less falsehoods
than half truths, as his life seems more a half-
    life now, as unapproachable as he,
further along wherever that firm step, stick
    and scowl led to or trailed from.
Forget pity, blame, his crumpled body in
    the stairwell, forget not asking
remember me? Forget burdens. Penance
    shifts and chafes like memory.

For a Liar

Volunteer little, suggest
less, be guided by the one
who questions you like a good
dance partner. If confronted
deny, and only if denial fails,
lie. Let a taste for elegant
simplicity decide, remembering
like a carpenter that details
are occasions for failure, like
a traveler, that each junction's
a point at which you must recall
the way you went and may get lost.
Think of a story as a bed of nails
that shreds unpracticed memory.

Admit whatever you have to,
but even the smallest changes are
the interest you should not
depend on, and your principal—
whatever no one is sure of. If
your inventions fade like cheap
yard goods, reuse them. It's true
the flamboyant sometimes survive
on mother wit and a quick tongue,
that the embroiderers scrape by
so long as no one is looking close,
and politicians, well whole careers
have been launched with smears
and slurs that circle like satellites.

Most lies, though, resemble pets
we give homes to and expect to be
loved by, the threadbare clothes we
assume compliment us. They're
improbable futures the stock markets
and lotteries make money on, demeaning
like chances we feel slip away. As
with other kinds of hope, they look

better than nothing when nothing looks
grim. The liar, too much a believer
in self-reliance, goes on shoring up
this with that until he comes up
one piece short, and with no one to
turn to, has to lie to himself.

Splinter

When a piece of it
caught on the third finger of my
right hand, then broke off as the rest
slid forward, I choked my howl, preferring
as I rose, to hop to the window
in the pink swell of morning

light, and pull. But you can tell
when you've left something behind,
and even then I'd started
rubbing one finger over the other, feeling
for it with blunt tweezers, because
a small annoyance is a constant

reminder some work's waiting. That night
I dug for treasure with a needle,
hacking till my hide resembled chopped
meat, almost convinced pain
was an echo of a pick clanging
in the mountains. I should have

weighed my chances, should have
left the work to that bundle
of pains and wants that hangs out
with my bones. The skin
healed over, leaving, like tailings,
the small hill a finger was sure to brush.

So I gave up, compressed the two sides
till the splinter, less than a quarter-inch
and almost translucent, slid out
on pus. The body brooks no invaders.
It surrounds, floats and when
the lucky break comes, fires them

through the surface
like rockets. That's how I learned it
and believed before cancer
and viruses and how we turn on ourselves,
thwarted hatred burning holes
in the gut, the pressure of blood

bursting through clogged arteries.
This was a splinter though,
sheathed in a ropy veil of dead white
cells, a shrouded, pale remembrance
of the outside returned
after my body finished with it.

The Escape

Amused when she asks, *is your wife Jewish?* and,
because it's easier, because I don't
want to think, I answer yes. It's the first time.
Later, a pushy man wants to know my
son's birthday. Confused, I make him younger
and the shift of dates feels so natural

I let it stand. Then it's happening with family
names, with where I work, how long, with
whom—minor changes in my *vita*, small alterations,
other lives, one variant for this person,
another for that, as though I were picking out
ballpoint pens or books, rummaging for

keepsakes to give away, a different self to
each, each time. Months pass before I
catch on too and admit I've done what I did out of
caution, an attempt to screen the self,
erase the scent, obscure the trail with a series
of deadends until no one could thread

a way through those dense thickets back to
me, reeking of fear. What did I think I
had worth hiding and who was I trying to deceive?
Tell me: surrounded by those casual lies
fabricated with disarming aplomb, why didn't I ask
whose escape I imagined I was fashioning?

Returning Home

The blinds already scribble black and white
on a day whose sage and powdery loam
seem to swell with remembered cars, jackhammers,
an afternoon air so waterlogged it's
like being wrapped in steamy towels. Faces
return, already touched with lies
on their way to dinner stories, the opalescent
sheen retelling lends a wave.

And although now, on a branch of the four story
pine I planted, a stellar's jay,
Mister Homebody, chuckles, I could turn from
a ship's rail, return to my cabin.
I scan the table for keys, trying to recall
which pocket to put them in, eyes
reddened like a drunk who can't find something
he remembers looking for,

who slides a dime back and forth, who keeps
going to keep going. If I had woken
to a splashing downpour, the cobbles shining,
it would only be another morning, though
in that place. One week I resolve to avoid some
room I pop up in like a bubble, and
the next, to stop dreaming. I'm the wind's,
swept away continuously, no loyalty

larger than a bird's, so unapproachable my wife
and son swear they hear me ticking.
Mirrors flow with my lives which have opened
a shy petal at a time and seemed, each
one, my one and only. They're the abandoned family
I kept turning to as, here, I say,
come to Papa, gathering in their adoring ooh's
and aah's, pink-edged as sunsets.

III

Morning Run

Isn't this morning's light over the valley
like thread, you said, and we set out early,
you with the dog, me ten minutes behind,
trucks digging the clumped, white sandstone
from the roadside ditches and the lights

still on in some of the cars headed to work.
The river shone. A heron flapped to one side—
ravens, ospreys above a territory the absolute
black and white of their chevroned wings marked.
Something I had to do later nudged and pulled

the sky behind like the roar of the diesel
in the loader or the truck starting to move off
under its cargo. Stirrings of wind fluttered
and the ridge we'd turned our backs on stacked
gray clouds like breakers. Keeping to the road

was hard, and heading back and heating up.
Even the brush of the envelope of air we were
part of would seem rare as that light, thickened
before we were home, as though obstacles,
unnoticed in passing, already had changed us.

The Proud

If the proud are wearing suits
of light like matadors, the bull, a stand-in
for misfortune, then metaphors must be their capes,
the big one turning him and the small
that brings the tips of the horns in close
and slices a layer of air just over the heart
clenching like fists the proud will raise soon,

flags of victory. Take the notion
the bull can only look forward to a good death
once he's been in the ring ten or fifteen minutes,
having learned too much for any future
matador—as if too much thought
were the picador, or the frilled darts he places
in the bull's thick, drooping neck, shreds of cloth

everyone wants some of, like the dignity
or honor we hope to cover our nakedness with,
should it come to that. Think how hard
the humble work at being meek, modest, even
servile, something that comes naturally
to the defeated, of the difference between
studying a language and acquiring it.

Think of those unable to afford
pride, the distorted features of those less concerned
with deportment—or the bull, which is not
misfortune but is only touched by it, as clothes
acquire our shapes in time. When the time comes
to show who they are, even the proud
will have to shed their pride,

along with their dignity perhaps
as we will have to stop arguing, confusion
almost total by then, the bulls running down
streets and the proud looking for benches to sit
or stand on. When the mood disperses,
festive or humdrum, and we return
to our habitual selves like row houses, how
will we distract the evasions we live by?

Karaites of Vilnius

i.

In Vilnius a woman tells the Germans come to collect her
she's a Karaite, not a Jew, though the dictionary calls Karaites
"a Jewish sect that rejected the Talmud in favor of the Torah."
Forty years pass like breathing in and out and she mentions it
to a friendly visitor who tells me: she said every Karaite in Vilnius
was spared—Karaites exotic where Jews were numerous
and rounded up and shuffled off to that gas which blew away.
Then what still hovers like a legendary smoke?

ii.

I always pictured Karaites as a part of Persia's warm downtowns,
pistachios, streets lined with trees that tremble, and a delicacy
so privileged, people avert their eyes, hum and busy themselves
at any required work. But in Vilnius, luck might consist of a ring
or cow, a chicken or a friend, not really close, to buy your life with.
It was cold with the chill that follows recognition. People froze
and scales swayed endlessly: who sold whom, sold out, bought
what with whom and at what price?

iii.

The Soviets turned off the gas to Vilnius one year when I was close
and history grew gravid with a shame like the frost that touched
the grapevine outside my house last night. Its bronze-like hands
shone this morning, till my touch shattered them. The Karaites
repudiated demons as "human imaginings." Therefore,
no demons live in Lithuania—or Karaites or their Talmudic
    neighbors,
too poor for gas, and what gleams there is like the slick,
now blank and cold, that follows innocence.

Home

When Eve awoke, there was a man
beside her, sleeping—this was before
fear and danger—like and unlike her,
lying on his side. She began
to hum and primp. Out of the blue
a breeze rose and fell in time
with the swing of his breathing, everything new

and yet, somehow, familiar. She stretched
her arm. He seemed to shudder then,
roll over, start as his eyes opened.
She was quiet. Maybe they watched
each other and there were no words
as there were no memories. Their lips brushed
accidentally as a cloud-burst

sends water down an empty channel,
and he rose and she rose, separately.
As they started walking off, he
waited or she did, until
they were in step, side by side, alone.
They approached the trees, saw between them
a path to follow and started home.

Wave, Bill

for William Stafford, two years dead

1.

We'd go looking for the right words
but you'd get up earlier and wait
till something would insinuate
itself behind the sounds we heard
and claim it was worth searching for—
like a line in grass the wind draws.

You'd set out the way coffee scents
a room, by drifting. Maybe you'd crack
the door for light and a line back
to your end would open. Patience
rewards because the world's boundless
for us as surely as any sound is,

and in time, everything comes wandering by.
Who will confuse us with simplicity?
Our losses dull us. There are two less
canny ears for the news on the wind now,
and no one half as sly to sing it back.

2.

Long ago, when I passed
an open window where you sat writing,
curtains pulled back to catch the morning,
you raised your head and waved. Wave to me
now. Toward the end, you seemed only
a little lost, a little thrown by deaths when
they started to pile up.

When they came too close,
you said, writing's not so important;
there are other things. Probing, sparring
again—or were you winding down, just
starting to turn off lights, lock doors, turn
your head and listen through that silence
you couldn't talk to?

Releasing a Bird

I've been working all of ten minutes when I hear
scraping, chewing, maybe a crunch, a flutter
in the ceiling, and finally recognize it: a bird
caught in the chimney pipe. I wait. No use.
I yank out the bottom-plate. He drops, black
fanning in all directions, flicker one

with crow at this point, and bangs into windows, one
after another. I open what opens, chase him here
and there till he's out the door, heart aflutter,
and soaring over the scrub-willows. Time to block
the chimney cap, I decide. Who wants birds
dropping in forever? So I climb up, use

an old plastic flower pot, then use
the height to scan the horizon, having won
that right by my good deed. Higher than the birds,
white cumulous clouds billow and spill. Here
it's bright, but you can make out shadows and black
thunderheads in the distance. My mood, the flutter

of good will, flag of my disposition, flutters,
sputters, slackens and droops. The ladder I used
to climb down with I can put away in the back,
and in the cabin I can sit at my desk, one
foot up, slowly rolling back the morning, hear
the parade of sounds and listen to the birds

outside, their commentless unfolding of bird-
song or hoot. But something's gone so utterly,
destabilizing, wrong, my mood slips. I hear
it reel, its scratching attempt to hold on, no use
once the slide begins, like the bird, gone
and not coming back if it knows what's good for it, soot-black,

storm-cloud-black, starling-black and back
there, somewhere in the distance that's blurred
now, that bright light has turned wan
and the bright mood muted, subdued, frittered
away now. What is it happiness doesn't like in us
that it can't stick around? What was here is there

and that's that. Some light's gone the way birds
fly south come winter's flutterings. You push your hair
back. You muse. You start thinking back.

Private Languages

What if we're always changing our minds
a little, simplifying a complex thought here,
dropping a qualification there, like speakers
still learning the language? Maybe we're
predestined to become our own models,
like the man recovering from stroke learning
to walk—hip-thrust, leg-swing, lock, weight down,
crumbling when he gets the sequence wrong.

Would we defy ontology, the imperfect imagining
perfection? If there were no private languages,
from what would public ones start? Assume
we had words to explain ourselves, to describe
places we'd never seen, people it was unlikely
we'd see again—the day past the one we knew
there was no coming back from. Would they be
enough for jokes? Say music spoke our emotions

in the hokey dialects we'd thought we outgrew
or shed like rumblings, heart murmurs, and we were
wrong from birth. Articulation might sculpt
air, an offering and its limit. That ongoing
affection for vowels—couldn't it start here—
for long O's and U's, the high E's which pierce
the circle of an open mouth, that flotsam
of bubbles and buoyed clouds that rise from us?

The Second Coming

They come looking like Latinos, dark
hair, dark eyes, air of poverty, that
slight build, those stoop-shoulders:
one turns to another, there's a dip,
a shrug and who they are is clear—
or like Native Americans, till one smiles
to another, and in his bewildered eyes,
rheumy with terror, you see history—
or like Chinese, clubby, having sneaked
in someplace they don't belong. One
lifts a fist heavenward, pounds his heart
and you've no doubt who's there. They're

a Conga line snaking, heel-and-toeing
forward toward you, smelling of garlic,
smelling of matches-herring, a troop
with dripping noses and wailing babies,
yours. And your house is so clean,
you're sure they'll ask themselves in
for the night because these ones are not
Latinos or Native Americans or Chinese
but your ones, old Jews from the Pale,
Litvoks, *Galitsianas*, and why they've
come and where they're going, you
don't have the right or chutzpah to ask.

The Light in the Hall

for Irina

Past eighty, she carried one suitcase stuffed
with clothes, and a bag with a tablecloth that weighed
forty years—too much and not enough.
There was a crossword she couldn't finish, a frayed
    passport in a pouch inside a dress
    she'd sewed herself. Her loss was bottomless.

She couldn't walk a block for bread
without hearing bullets ricocheting there,
in Tbilisi. Words rebound, the sounds as dead
as traffic noises here. Her lap dog bares
    its stubby yellow teeth, then coughs
    its life away. And when it drifts off

like a rowboat someone forgot to tie,
the need for blankets to muffle its night-long bouts
of coughing vanish like annoyance, dry-
eyed and sleepy. Only a fool would doubt
    she's better off, only a graceless
    native say so to her face.

Her suitcase won't close, a paradox
to puzzle stay-at-homes. Under the bed
it grows heavy as if filled with rocks
or mountains and the skyline that said
    welcome home. The light in the hall
    says: the stairs start here, don't fall.

End of the Season

for Steve Smith

We'd gotten onto the water late, the two of us
crammed in that raft, the sun
low in the sky to start with,
so I should have known better than stopping
so often, even if the fishing was slow
and had to get better. When the great horned owl
touched down not fifty feet off, watching us
fish one spill, and held still atop his rock
in the shallows, turning
flat face, yellow eyes and no neck
with the sluggishness of royalty as he followed us
past, I should have begun catching on:
the stops were surges of hope
that let our hearts dart erratically
like bats we were starting to see. Nothing
would work. We'd catch a few small trout, but this was fall,
time for the big ones before the season ran out. Now
or never, I thought, casting
baetis flies smaller than matchheads,
splashing stoneflies, dragging and spluttering an orange caddis
through the riffles. Nothing
worked. And by the time we realized nothing
was going to work we'd squandered our chances
of day light. I was worrying
how to navigate through the downed trees and sweepers
in the dark and you, fretting we might miss
signs of the dam. Cold twisted up
our legs like vines, each of us deep in his own version
of trouble and the moon no help, not high
or full enough to cast light
on the narrow current we were part of.

Quail in February

The heads of the quail jerk mechanically
across the ice-crusted snow, absurd
crests bobbing, feet speeding, like a movie
run too fast, when the covey, each bird
inflating it, collected now, stops short
on a patch of bare ground.
Under a gnarled sagebrush, they cavort
solemnly turning around and around,

then dip, pecking at anything resembling food,
gray, faded feather-balls, and at once are gone,
having heard above them a rattling at the altitude
of harm. As if struck, they explode, abandon
ground, fired off like barrages of arrows,
rigid, whistling, gliding
to the next hawk-proof thicket, strutting below
a hatchwork of branches in folded wings.

Fishing

When the river rushes by, you seem to step
onto another shore. Never mind
you were always there: now the hum and grind
of all you seemed to hear shuts down. You've let

a door close, tall, transparent. You've crossed a line
that glimmered. Now the water sparkles. Hawks
spiral up and swallows bend from the sky
to rake the surface. When the moon's chalky

face looks down later, when the friend on the phone
sounds thick from work or drink, that quiet comes
back. The fish were always iridescent.

One floats up to a fly and you're alone,
on one bank where night's the other. For a moment,
your breath sticks, waiting for the world's return.

Hunting

for Joe

I'm leaning in Joe's doorway
a little the way clouds behind his head
slouch into Table Mountain, allowing
as how my son has said, you can't always tell
where they're going to land
after you shoot them
and how I'd yelled back, about the three ducks
he'd left to rot, you don't shoot
unless you can. Joe is sitting
at his desk, head
tipped up to catch my words
as I repeated my son's
lame excuse: he couldn't get into
the trunk where the raft was, and anyway
he hadn't known they'd drop
on the other side of a pond which was fenced off
and besides, Joe once told him sometimes it happens.
I leave out my screaming that I didn't give a damn
what Joe said. When Joe asks
if we'll be home Christmas vacation
and maybe he'll take the two boys hunting,
it's all I can do
to let it seem conversation on a cloudy day. So
Joe's saying he sided with me, and this year
he'd almost not gotten a license,
remembering being eleven with a cow elk permit.
He'd spotted one, dropped her
with one shot, crossed all
but ten feet of the clearing
when she raised her head and looked at him

with those big brown eyes, what I call
a look that says, "something's
wrong, Doctor, I'm so glad you're here." But I'm
city and Joe, raised to hunt,
kept going and shot her through the head,
only she managed to raise it
once more, the dislocated jaw dragging at an angle.
That's when he'd fled.
His father cut her throat
and gutted her—"They're such hunters, my family."

Rabbit

He's the brown patch beyond the window
    that hasn't greened up yet,
nibbling fresh shoots and set off by a clump
    of cheatgrass. Unaware
that he's been spotted, he bends to his eating,
    freezing at a jay's call,

long, furry ears atwitter as if a breeze fluttered,
    flattening them suddenly,
then, slow as a sponge reconstituting itself,
    upright again, he's breathing.
Rabbit's the heroic victim, able to make
    a break for it while quaking,

mobile, though afraid. Even how he hops
    off when you sneak up, rigid,
twitches then, exploding past his own shoulder
    almost, tells you how hard he
hopes to escape you, but wags the snowy flag
    of his butt just in case.

A Legend of Moses

When Moses, having killed the overseer,—brothers
  intent on betraying him complaining "who
appointed you over us,"—flees Egypt, we anticipate
  blind soldiers who can speak and seeing
ones who can't, the classic pairings of confusion,
  and some cave or other where he hides,

though the Bible is silent. We know the telling
  must be shortened since a story requires
space for unfolding its slightly altered frames
  which give the illusion of movement and,
as with a tree's growth, differ so little one from
  the next that those close by never notice.

There will be commentaries. Moses can be lost
  from view a while as the tale flees south
and ground is prepared in Kush between magicians,
  conflicts years long littered with battles.
Moses will reappear as the king he so much is that
  even benighted people freely chose him.

We yearn for the omissions. Even in the mind's fields,
  events leave trails, and trails wander
hill and dale as we do, though if you had
  to fight a battle or conclude a peace
on time instead of only having to arrive at the end,
  you might throw up your hands as listeners do.

In the Midrashim, Moses has the strength of lions,
  the swiftness of eagles, yet it's foresight—
unnoted, his storks that eat the magician's snakes
  in the final battle,—that gives his armies
victory. How did he know and where did he learn
  to raise such birds? He rules forty years.

The teller, whether the story he tells is one he lived
   in the land of tick and tock or of somewhere
else where time's measuring rod is marked differently,
   must select this from that and keep us
following, until we think we see how one turn connects
   or echoes another to foreshadow that symmetry

and balance so pleasantly soothing we give it place
   and time in our world too. Something small
is gnawing, rubbing. It irritates like a frayed nail,
   a loose thread. Whether we clip or unravel it,
the same gap appears. Two pieces didn't meet flush,
   didn't hook, snap or join. In a tree,

this would be where the disease started, in armor,
   the point to aim an arrow or ax at. In assaults
on ourselves, it marks a crack; doubt wedges an entrance
   where hunger infiltrates the story. How
did we get from there to here? The miraculous rod
   created in the twilight of the first Sabbath Eve,

which Moses brings Jethro, suggests the Red Sea. There's
   this too: when he turns Tzipporah, who is his wife,
and his sons, Gershom and Eliezer, south, though the written
   text moves invariably north and east, they enter
its gaps like furry clouds above a river, the smoke
   of sacrifice, all our cooling breath.

Rest

The sky lies on the river,
on its fall-thickened surface
like breath, a heavy palm that's flattened out
every feature. Here and there
the moving water washes, molds itself
above and around rock, plastic, continuous,

seamlessly uninterruptible and ruptureless,
which is the way the sky is,
leaden today, cloudless. In silence,
only the rush of water, friction and slippage
as it rounds a bank, as it drops
inches over stones into a new pool.

The purlings, the simple gulpings
that turn up air and whiten in
the process, are they impatience?
And if not for this radiance, if
not for the monotone of two halves
mirroring each other, neither source

nor primary, not even a note of trembling—
for what? That steel-gray is sky and water
two ways, and so icy it's left
little frozen ledges that will melt
in an hour—as the shore will,
as the rest. Rest too.

IV

Dent

Late in the morning,
clouds building in gray stacks in the west
and the wind kicking up, bowing the trees,
sending sheets of sand and dirt across the street
I see the smashed rear door-skirt,
the dent in the car, which my wife told me
a friend's son had done but which she hadn't seen
clearly in the evening light and thought was small—
metal crumbled in and discolored
like a bruise. It will rust.
The car looks like trash,
I tell her, another piece of junk.
She's already in action,
calling the insurance company, car company,
friend. But later, when I've half stacked
a cord of wood and she comes to tell me
what they've said and I've told her
the car will run anyway, it's nothing major,
some money at most, she asks me why I blamed her.
But I didn't, see, I was just depressed
and what she heard was something different,
as now I remember her way of talking about a dragonfly,
a jewel of a creature, four inches long, the black
tube of its body dotted turquoise;
there it was in the gravel making the rattling
I had heard, that drew me to it, and made me
call her out, not rising, beating transparent wings
then stopping. I think it's dying, I said, and she
pointed to the missing wing and said, "poor thing."
Assuming, of course, she thought it could feel
the loss or sense the future, I was certain
that was wrong for a creature like that, false
sympathy, I thought, when all she'd done
was voice her regret.

Teleologist

For my friend Bob there is only one
question, *why*, and two responses:
blame those involved and/or uncover
the unstated interest at bottom. He's
not fooled by mere appearances, this
teleologist, believer in conspiracies,
cabals, the dark and smoky rooms where
plotters plot the downfall of all they
disagree with and so violently, their
dark hearts fill with revenge, and hate

reigns like a queen. And since Bob,
my friend, sees hypocrisy rather than
moral outrage at work, he's convinced
they hound the President and hold him
to inappropriate standards. If there's
an action, someone's behind it, he
thinks, a self-styled rationalist and,
perhaps, the last paid-up subscriber
to the argument from design, though
he views these designers as malevolent,

malicious and, by extrapolation,
always afraid. Thus, because he is
a thoughtful man, though given to
strong feelings and passions that can
and have swept him away, and since
what drives him has been known to
push him past what he recalls as
reasons for his feelings or himself
or neither, leaving him flailing
hands big as pink, marble-veined

hams and flapping a sharp tongue,
powered by bellow-like lungs
that filled more than one room
with such vituperation it seemed
all the bricks and brickbats from
the well-stoked ovens of hell had
come crashing down around your

unprotected head—because he
believes in even if he does not
practice the efficacy of reason,

Bob can know with unshakable
conviction that those responsible
for the hounding of a John Locke
and the distortion of the thought
of Georg Wilhem Friedrich Hegel
are just those who fear a reason
which supports freedom, democracy
and the other goods he takes to be
unassailably, first principal *desiderata*.
Maybe it's the unfairness of that

and the destructive meanness implied
that drives him to dissect their dirty-
work, if only so no perpetrator can
hide behind it. His own bulk signals
an immoderation of style and fervor
he favors while joining the remainder
of who he is to a thunder usually
associated with the Biblical prophets,
John Brown and men on four-step
aluminum ladders, unfurled flags

behind, thumping the leather covers
of their Bibles as they point long fingers
and wait for the ground to open up
and swallow a heckling female or child—
and points as well to some terrible
unhappiness no by-pass surgery,
crude psychologizing or nitro pills
can touch, so intrinsic it's unreachable,
unextractable and likelier than enemies
he's unknown to, to gobble him up.

Soutine's Studio

Red burns from two directions: within the canvas,
threatening, and with a sting, here.
If you have to ask about power, skip kings
and try the man picking garbage,
his sour kids. Better yet, get down on all fours,
a scrubwoman at daily prayer, and suffer it
like the passions that master you, lashing you along
roads they choose. The trees may arch
above; keep moving. Later, a stringy bellboy,

tipped maybe, may stride from a shadow
that looks sky-blue, but sheathes him head to toe
in feigned contempt. And above a stove,
the bent pastry *sous-chef*, chalky moon face dripping,
may only seem skewed. Can you picture
his salute? Not just glowing carcasses, sides of beef
or stippled chickens, lumpy, dangling
from nailheads headfirst: paint itself has to
stink to high heaven. Chaim Soutine deals

in cash. If he can lay it out for paint and brushes,
you can bathe, dress, and climb his dirty
stairs holding your nose. Gawk, haggle: it won't
change the canvases he'll burn tomorrow.
They're meat his ulcers eat, wounds that torch
the roads lined green. They'll ripen; he'll
be rushed to Paris, too late to cut or run.
What kills a man are trees that lean
too close, villages that sway and won't stay put.

Snow

Snow's falling, already cold
from falling so long, all
the freshness of it, like white
hair, old news, all that's under it, quiet.
The sky bleaches, the hills

leach out while snow
slants in one window
and, like a sigh, sinks
in another. Explain how
rain does the same thing

to the dog dipping her snout,
shoveling up drifts, powder
almost leaping in air she's after,
snapping at it, and the river
drinking it in. Who can be sure

each flake's unique or tastes
sharp and tinny? But could anyone
doubt snow's temporary?
Maybe that's the news
snow's so busy burying.

From the House

The arms of the darkened trees are filled
with the pitch and breathing of space.
When cars beyond them race
by, only leaves rustle, stalled
at the edge of your attention
like a peaceful marriage. How do we shun

so much when so much is fleeting? You know
what happens: a lack of trust
shows up as greed, lust,
erosion of concern—the growth
of slow but deadening cancers.
Maybe fate is a good boxer

with a one-two so fast it seems
only a one, but think
of trees, arms linked
above the strict horizon, how we lean
toward them, stretching to listen
from the house. It's as if voices begin,

intimate talk in another room
we seem never to enter.
The speeding cars litter
the roadside. They bring home
a loneliness so youthful or rare,
you forget to listen for its answer.

The trees might say it was yourself
transformed, always another
you sought, part lover
and ghost, a husband. Notice with what stealth
the moon turns its key
in the numbed branches, entering the sky.

All Right

He plops down in the chair, his meat
hanging from him, sacked eyes
drooping, even the webs that lie
between his fingers weighted. They beat him
back into his bedroom—his son,
his boarder, their friends—up to one
a.m. drinking beer and playing video
games on his tv each night.
He wants me to say, it's all right,

kick them all out. He needs
me to say, save yourself,
because he knows they won't and he's helpless,
likely to explode inside, sneeze
some thin walled blood vessel, maybe
in his poor brain, so that he
goes down in a puddle on the floor
swinging his massive arms before

help or cops arrive. What's harder
is the son who, like a plea from someone
drowning, pulls and will not take from
him anything but money and the house. And martyr
though he is, my friend knows that he needs
me to reassure him it's what he needs to
do. And because I'm his friend, I do.

Bulltrout

for Jim Spotts

A green, mote-filled light settles through Doug fir
and ponderosa pine that line the boulder-
choked stream we hike, long-handled nets for staffs
and probes. You wave a stop and point.
Tucked in by a jumble of snags, a bulltrout: the white
edge on the root-purple dorsal of
the male, all three tense feet of whip-quick muscle,

and, nearby, the sheltered female finning languidly.
You lean out for pictures and they dive
center-stream. The banks keep narrowing as we rise
and climb. The next pair's by a ledge
too bare to hide them, the couple after that, my eyes
adjusting to the spangled water, the coins
of light, are almost prominent. I try to scoop one,

and the fish, longer than my net is deep, flexes twice
then slaps back into the tumbling stream—water
so clear and frigid that when I take the inevitable misstep
and plummet to my chin between smooth rocks,
the smack is like a slap or shock. We flush another pair,
then the solitary male I do net and lift, red
stippling his orange belly and gray flank, huge hook or kype

and staring eye. He flails, gill plate smeared with blood.
When I tail him back in, he lies still, gasping
on the bottom stones, yawning as he revives. And I'm relieved
when he breaks for the foam below the boulders
and falls—one, you say, of less than fifty left. By then
I'm chattering, cold rattling me from my bones
outward toward our starting point, miles and years away.

Friendship seems a kind of obdurate trust, a cold purity
we sense can't live with us, yet have to
test until it changes into something else we count, take
the measure of and return. Or it becomes
the stream above a lake floor patrolled by huge shadows
more elemental than ours, only secure
as long as isolated. The green light pools like ice.

Writing Back

New Year's cards: pictures of Estonia's boulder strewn coast
  and feathery, black trees behind which waves
and patches of white gradually dissolve—the troika, its horses
  twisting in three directions, rearing, the peasant
about to be swept up, her yoke and pails scattered in snow.

It's almost February, and I'm just starting on lies that thicken
  my tongue, thanks where no thanks are due,
looking for that single, genuine detail around which to forge
  the requisite sincerity. When I set to work,
I know only that my writing back is starting a way back.

I think of the classroom and smell something I can't name.
  I see three students shuffle papers and wonder
how we will last the ninety minutes. Outside the window
  jackdaws sit in the wind-tossed branches, black
on black in a darkness already palpable by three p.m.

I'm walking back from the Hermitage, following marble
  palace building after building and the lights
glitter across the river and on the river, the classroom,
  here. I'm crossing the arched, stone bridge,
lanterns aglow, granite column floodlit in the snowy square.

Where's the shabby, cheerless room that awaits me? Who
  could want its loneliness? St. Isaac's glows,
the Admiralty clock faces glow. You don't have to know why.
  You do what we do. You don't have to know
which lines you set or drags or hooks or how the Neva flows.

The Suddenness of Beauty

A front door swings open and a man comes out,
or waiting for a bus, hair sopping, a woman
turns. And the sheer beauty of his face or hers

stops you like a wall or slap. Why here, you'd
appeal, if your tongue worked, why hasn't loveliness
lifted you out of the paper-littered streets

like wings, the rareness of it swept you toward
the polished cities and their rug-hushed rooms,
you almost ask, thrilled by the democracy of beauty.

What the rich, what the powerful overlooked, quickens
in an unselfconscious blossoming, as if the bud,
the furled banner, the folded parachute of it

was always about to burst into fullness, maybe
in a city you have not even thought to visit,
at the bus stop, beneath the next street lamp.

Homage: Variation on a Theme of Paul Celan

I hear that the axe has flowered,
I hear that the place can't be named,

I hear that the bread which looks at him
heals the hanged man,
the bread baked for him by his wife,

I hear that they call life
our only refuge.

—tr. Michael Hamburger

I hear that the books can be corrected,
I hear that the mistakes can be renamed

and that moles swim in dirt
and live lives of perfect commitment.

*   *   *

I hear that irony dries the tongue
and when autumn comes

the leaves fall, speech fails
and the tourists go home—

that the Seine, even when filthy, shines.

I hear there is another version
of the past in which no one is to blame.

*   *   *

I hear the defiled used to need us.
I hear that memory could replace justice once.

I hear that we can shut our eyes
and snow tucks the corpses in
like flattening rocks.

I hear there is another life
for which only we are responsible.

How Could You Know

Black and white, big red tongues lolling
to one side, the huskies are mushing ahead,
coming right for you from the trash-can side
under the unseen pulsing of the Northern
Lights. And from the radio, a disembodied
wind is flooding the room with sound. Bold
W's of crows above the far ridge, rain clouds
stacked higher and the weeds waving fistfuls
of dead, spiked flowers. It was still light
when three deer stepped from a thicket behind
the garden, approached the arbor—slow, lock-
step—lowered their heads and began to feed.
I remembered tomato plants, peppers, beans
and grape leaves nibbled back to the vine
in August. So I slid the sash and yelled, *out
of here, no dinner for you*, restrained, polite,
I thought. They went on with their business,
and when I stepped outside to discuss it with them
kept munching till I was no more than yards
away. The female, the closest, raised her eyes
then, clearly offended, the spike joined in
and the rest bounded off on loaded springs
while the dog I feed slept on. The huskies
on the feed can mushed forward, leaves rattled,
some clouds the sun had combed an hour before
spread across the sky behind them, black
by then, and the ridge was blazing gold.
The huskies seemed to hear someone calling:
good dogs all—like radio waves from Mars
or holes in all we think. Space grew more
palpable, limpid and the static rougher,
louder and the stars drew blood like salt.

Murmurs

I sit where the guest sits when language turns suddenly
opaque. It's me in the uncoupled car left
in the station as the train fades, me adrift
on voluble liquids, hushes—me at sea.

When distractions like meaning vanish, maybe you hear
murmurs the way doctors hear valves
rattle in the rush of heart's blood, the octaves
masked off or lying below speech and tears:

Tanya's unhappiness with Sergei, the extended complaint
that's replaced a life, places to dream about
and the despair that wears through then wears out
feeling. Without a segue, I'm in role, in accent.

Back on track, I'm in the harboring circle
of friends, pulling shoes on, doing a button,
ready for the long walk to the metro. *When
will you be back?* they ask. *Don't forget to call.*

Keriah

for Diane

1.

You pin the short strip of ribbon on
the left, over the heart for sister, son
and daughter—the right side for others, says
the rabbi, handing out the black badges
of mourning as he prays. *Traditionally,*
our people rent their clothes, strew ashes, he
explains, in a practiced voice, patient with us
who've hired him. All the while I'm drifting off,
thinking of my mother's body, anonymous
and cold somewhere, of this last act of love.

The rabbi walks up to my sister, lifts
a razor and with a stroke practiced, swift,
and accurate, makes a gash halfway through
the cloth, mumbles for each of us a few
words. When it's my turn, half expecting pain
or blood, I cringe, and am disappointed when
there's nothing. More explanation: *others will know*
you're to be treated carefully as you submit
to grief ... He drones on. I want sorrow
to hold and rock me. Or I want to hold it

in place of my mother's body which we chose
not to see. A brief service. At its close
we read short tributes, announce an "open house"
for friends and relatives. My sister counts
out forks, the food arrives. Light talk. The rabbi's
interested in poetry's surprise
and passion. Cousins linger. We sweep up, straighten
and stand out on the balcony, the moon
highlighting the Intercoastal's broken ribbon.

2.

I finished dressing with the torn,
black ribbon half beneath my vest—
visible, though not displayed. You saw,

if you looked, otherwise it was there
just for me, the way in a poem
I like to keep rhyme and meter.

When I moved, the kreeh would stay hidden
or show, but I would always know
the point of the pin skating lightly on

my skin—not enough to break through
and dot me with blood; rather pinpricks
of discomfort spreading like news

broadcasts, as if to call back
consciousness. That little pain
was insistent, like the clicking of a clock

yet quiet as salt that draws out a wine stain—
the edge we drive our pleasure past
in self-indulgence. When it was time

a month later to leave off
the kreeh, I missed it, but was ready.
I was more used to that absence of love

like a ringing or sting inside me.

Time as Distance

If time were a form of space, as we feel it must be,
then even the meeting of people born
fifteen years apart would require negotiating vast,
unfamiliar distances scored with chasms,
walled with forbidding mountains and any efforts
to broach them would seem heroic, even if they fell short.

We'd respect the travelers, no matter from which side
they arrived, but there'd always be something wrong
about them: a smell, a notion they hadn't thought to hide
that said plainly they didn't belong
and not just because they were different,
but some glibness when we shook, some fear in our merriment.

We'd consider their assumptions of what should or could
be shared as comic or tragic, some
idiosyncratic vagary of mood—
and proof they were tourists in a region
they'd read up on, with phrase books, prepared for the exotic
by wide tastes, and yet become quickly a little homesick.

Take the extremes: the young who can never learn
enough about what people did
in their evenings or would have, if they'd had time or a few coins
somehow cajoled from whoever hid
the meager supply, and the old who seem deaf
to the new world of sound they swim through and beneath.

So if mechanics assumes two things can't be
in the same place at the same time,
why not credit this variation: that two things can't be
in the same place from different times,
which is not quite an obverse, but makes its own
kind of sense, "at" and "from" in a clear disjunction.

The thing is, we are always having to choose
ourselves, the who we can't escape,
assigning importance to a game or ritual, the evening news,
the evening drink, because we're afraid
no one else will, and stamped on each of the endless
bricks that face in and surround us are dates like glyphs or cliffs.

Music

In the dirty city, the sun burns down
the west, the blacks of back-lit trees and fading
grays of apartments exhaust one another.
Among the children smoking, women
stooping to sweep or weep in their long hair,
and drunks who are weaving between their steps,

the fashionable girls weave their way
to the concert hall and its plush benches
where they can reach for another world,
maybe with its share of grief, but not the dirt
or crumbling bas-relief, the armless, the blind,
and signs saying a daughter has cancer or please

help me get bread. Music can lift them away,
though they cannot stay where it takes them,
as the sunset will not keep the lovely trees,
silhouettes now, from fading into a darkness
it seemed to forestall, which may have been
or played a part in its consuming beauty.

$$\frac{92}{93}$$

Acknowledgements

Versions of these poems appeared in the following publications:

Agni: "Returning Home"
Bayberry Review: "Fishing"
Caffeine Destiny: "Music"
Comstock Review: "Private Languages"
Courtland Review: "The Muse As Lilith," "Cold Comfort"
Crab Creek Review: "Wave, Bill"
Crazy Horse: "All Right"
Ergo: "Just the Light"
Green Mountain Review: "Splinter"
Iowa Review: "Orphans"
Laurel Review: "Yom Kippur Again"
Mid-American Review: "End of the Season"
Nebraska Review: "Dent," "Soutine's Studio"
NeoVictorian/Chochlea: "From the House"
New Stone Circle: "The Suddenness of Beauty"
Northwest Review: "Waiting," "Spinoza," "Abe Lincoln,
    The First Jewish President"
Notre Dame Review: "The Elegant Ladies of Tallinn,"
    "Easter Lilies"
Overthewall: "The Swedish Minister at Tartu," "Just the light,"
    "Hunting"
Ploughshares: "In Chekhov"
Poetry: "On the Steps of Temple Shalom"
Potlatch: "Variations on a Theme of Paul Celan"
Prairie Schooner: "Bulltrout," "Needs," "The Escape,"
    "Karaites of Vilnius"
San Diego Reader: "Morning Run," "Quail in February"
Seattle Review: "The Light in the Hall," "Writing Back,"
    "Murmurs"
Seneca Review: "Time as Distance"
Shenandoah: "A Legend of Moses"
Tar River Poetry Review: "For a Liar"
Yale Review: "Millennium"

Pontoon #2 (anthology of Washington State Poets 1998)
Floating Bridge Press: "The Good News," "Just the Light"

Pontoon #3 (anthology of Washington State Poets 1999)
Floating Bridge Press: "For a Liar," "In Chekhov,"
"The Muse as Lilith"

Mark Halperin received a BA in physics from Bard College, worked as a junior research physicist, then studied philosophy at the New School for Social Research while employed as an electron microscope technician. Later, he received an MFA in poetry from the University of Iowa. Presently, he teaches in the English Department at Central Washington University. He has taught in Japan, Estonia, Russia (St. Petersburg), and was a Fulbright lecturer at Moscow State Linguistic University.

His three other volumes of poetry are *Backroads* (University of Pittsburgh Press), *A Place Made Fast* (Copper Canyon Press), and *The Measure Of Islands* (Wesleyan University Press). He has published translations from the poetry and prose of Soviet-period and contemporary Russian writers. Halperin received Glasscock, International Poetry Forum, and Washington State Artists Trust awards. He enjoys playing traditional music on banjo and guitar, as well as fly-fishing the Yakima River, near which he lives with his wife, the painter Bobbie Halperin.

New Issues Poetry & Prose

Editor, Herbert Scott

James Armstrong, *Monument in a Summer Hat*
Michael Burkard, *Pennsylvania Collection Agency*
Anthony Butts, *Fifth Season*
Gladys Cardiff, *A Bare Unpainted Table*
Lisa Fishman, *The Deep Heart's Core Is a Suitcase*
Joseph Featherstone, *Brace's Cove*
Robert Grunst, *The Smallest Bird in North America*
Mark Halperin, *Time as Distance*
Myronn Hardy, *Approaching the Center*
Edward Haworth Hoeppner, *Rain Through High Windows*
Janet Kauffman, *Rot* (fiction)
Josie Kearns, *New Numbers*
Maurice Kilwein Guevara, *Autobiography of So-and-so:
    Poems in Prose*
Lance Larsen, *Erasable Walls*
David Dodd Lee, *Downsides of Fish Culture*
Deanne Lundin, *The Ginseng Hunter's Notebook*
Joy Manesiotis, *They Sing to Her Bones*
David Marlatt, *A Hog Slaughtering Woman*
Paula McLain, *Less of Her*
Malena Mörling, *Ocean Avenue*
Julie Moulds, *The Woman with a Cubed Head*
Marsha de la O, *Black Hope*
C. Mikal Oness, *Water Becomes Bone*
Elizabeth Powell, *The Republic of Self*
Margaret Rabb, *Granite Dives*
Rebecca Reynolds, *Daughter of the Hangnail*
Martha Rhodes, *Perfect Disappearance*
John Rybicki, *Traveling at High Speeds*
Mark Scott, *Tactile Values*
Diane Seuss-Brakeman, *It Blows You Hollow*
Marc Sheehan, *Greatest Hits*
Phillip Sterling, *Mutual Shores*
Angela Sorby, *Distance Learning*
Russell Thorburn, *Approximate Desire*
Robert VanderMolen, *Breath*
Martin Walls, *Small Human Detail in Care of National Trust*
Patricia Jabbeh Wesley, *Before the Palm Could Bloom:
    Poems of Africa*